1st Recital Series

FOR MALLET PERCUSSION

Including works of:
- James Curnow
- Craig Alan
- Mike Hannickel
- Ann Lindsay

Solos for Beginning
through Early Intermediate
level musicians

CURNOW®
M U S I C

EXCLUSIVELY DISTRIBUTED BY

HAL•LEONARD®
CORPORATION

7777 W. BLUEMOUND RD. P.O. BOX 13819 MILWAUKEE, WI 53213

Edition Number: CMP 0857.03

1st Recital Series
Solos for Beginning through Early Intermediate level musicians
Piano Accompaniment for Mallet Percussion

ISBN: 978-90-431-1924-5

Foreword

High quality solo/recital literature that is appropriate for performers playing at the Beginner through Early Intermediate skill levels is finally here! Each of the **1st RECITAL SERIES** books is loaded with exciting and varied solo pieces that have been masterfully composed or arranged for your instrument.

Included with the solo book there is a professionally recorded CD that demonstrates each piece. Use these examples to help develop proper performance practices. There is also a recording of the accompaniment alone that can be used for performance (and rehearsal) when a live accompanist is not available. A separate solo Mallet Percussion book is available [edition nr. CMP 0853.03].

Table of Contents

MALLET PERCUSSION

1. KAITLIN'S MUSIC BOX

Ann Lindsay (ASCAP)

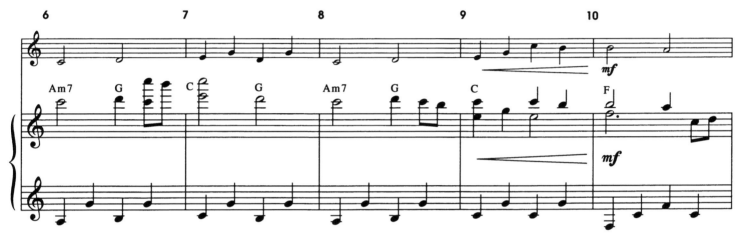

2. THE KOI POND

Craig Alan (ASCAP)

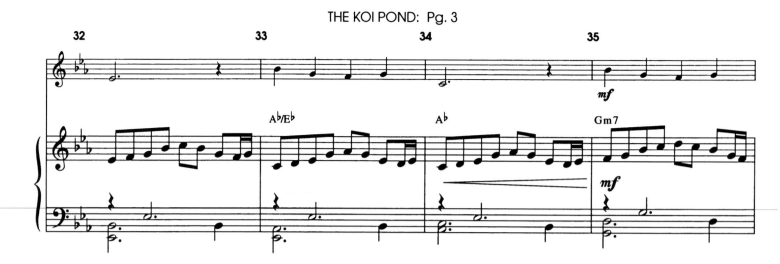

W.D.Bradbury and C. Elliott
3. JUST AS I AM
Arr. **Mike Hannickel** (ASCAP)

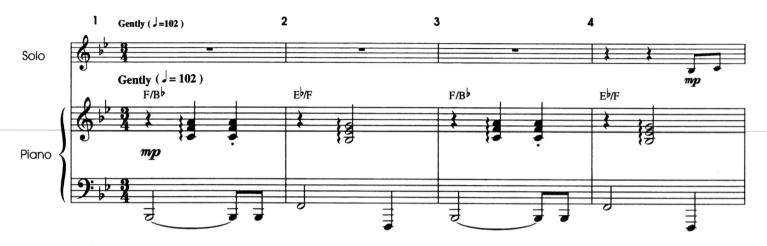

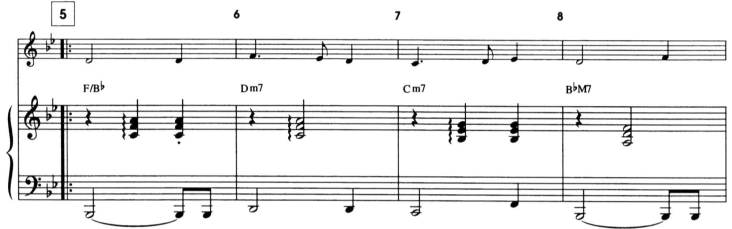

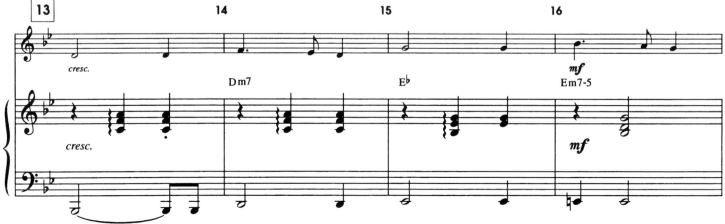

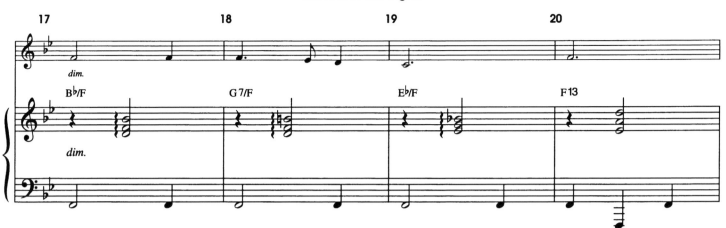

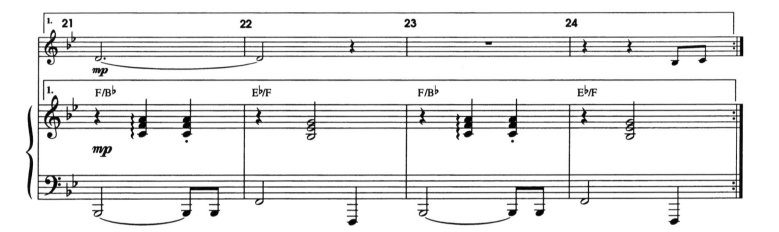

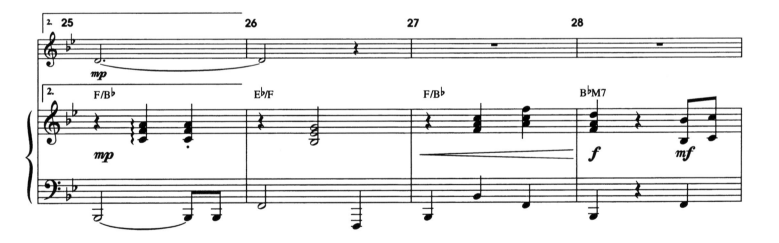

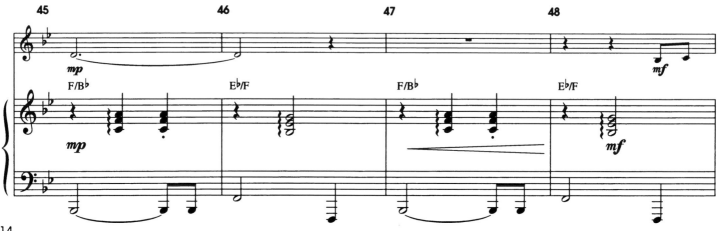

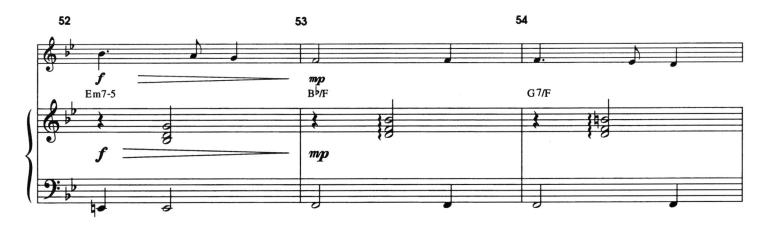

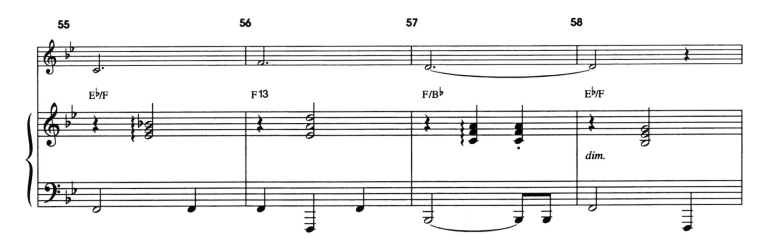

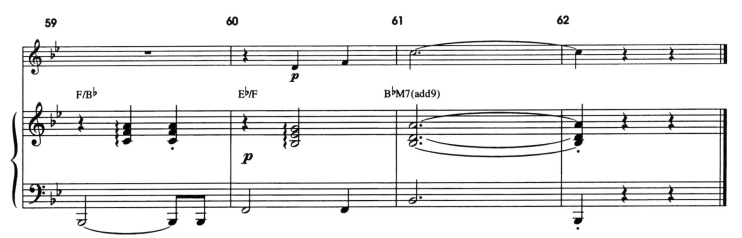

Jacques Offenbach

4. THE CAN-CAN

MALLET PERCUSSION

Arr. **Craig Alan** (ASCAP)

16

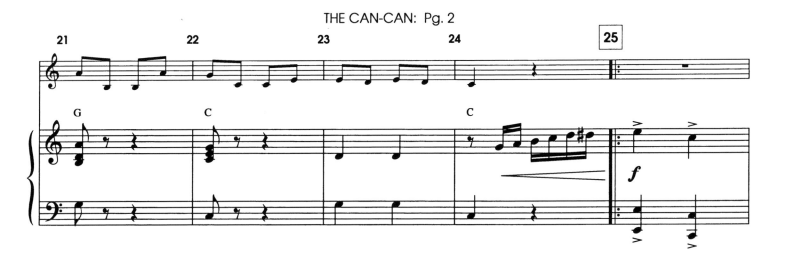

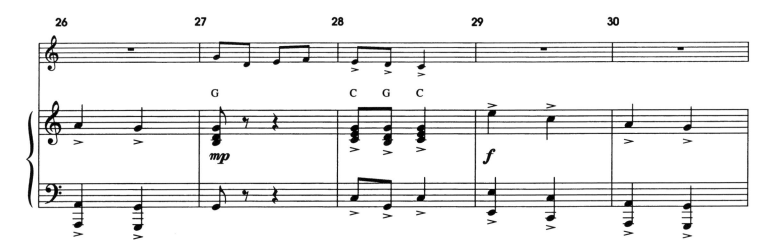

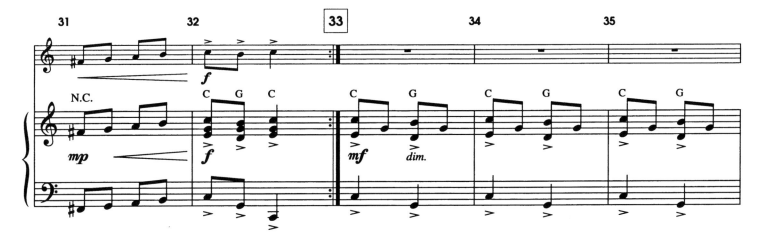

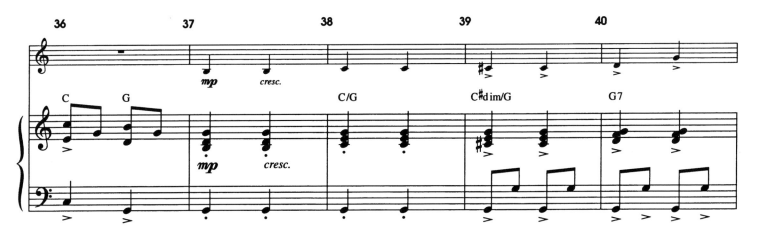

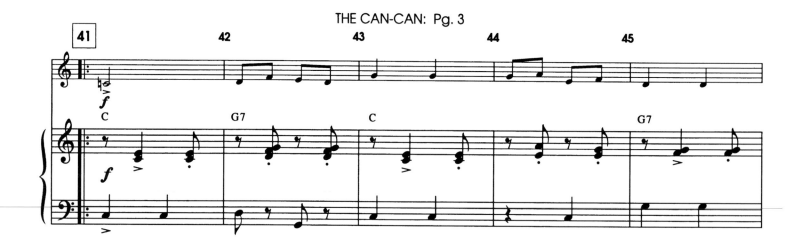

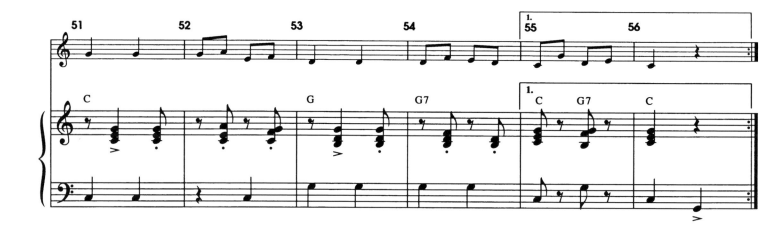

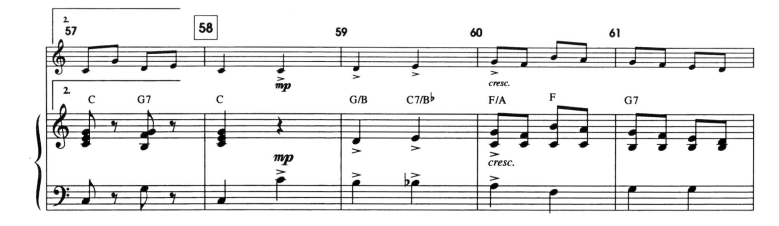

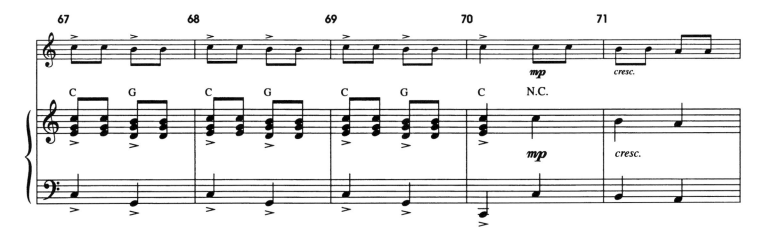

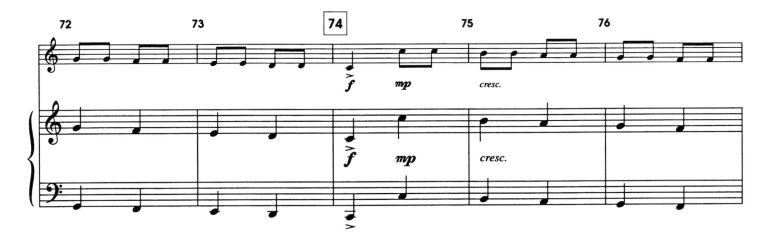

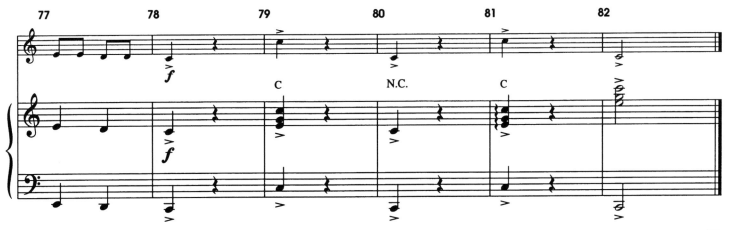

5. GRANDFATHER'S CLOCK

MALLET PERCUSSION

Arr. **Mike Hannickel** (ASCAP)

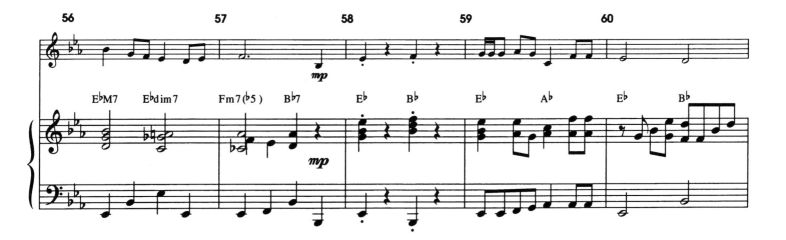

Scott Joplin

6. THE ENTERTAINER

Arr. **Ann Lindsay** (ASCAP)

MALLET PERCUSSION

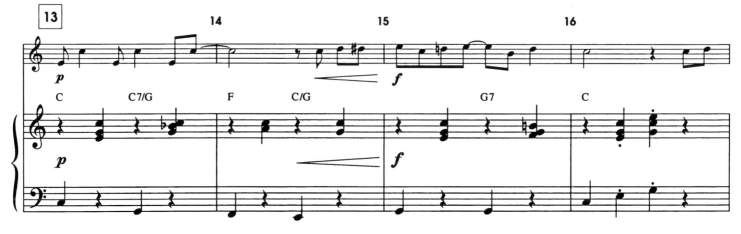

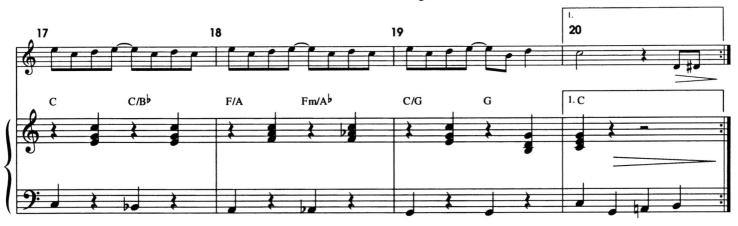

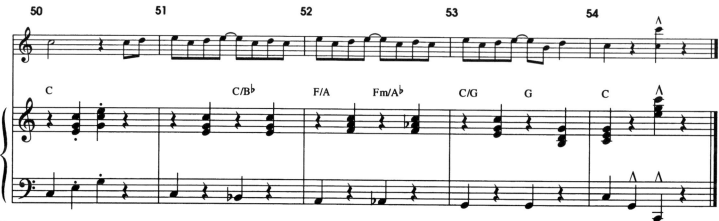

J.S. Bach
7. ARIOSO
Arr. Craig Alan (ASCAP)

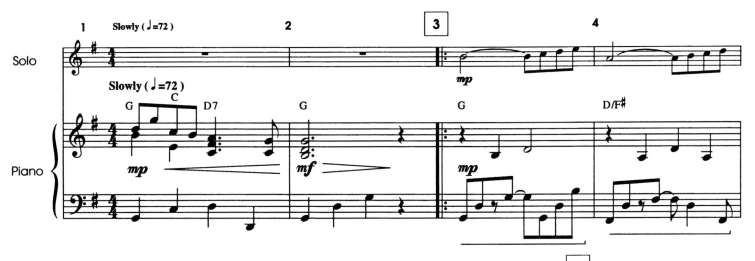

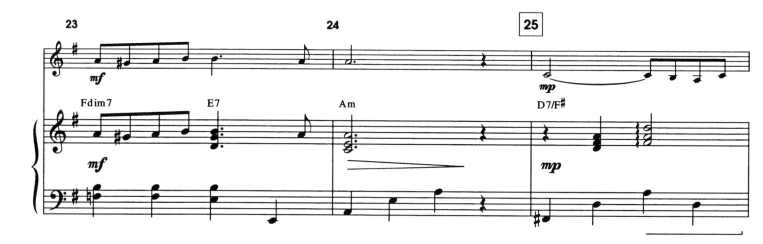

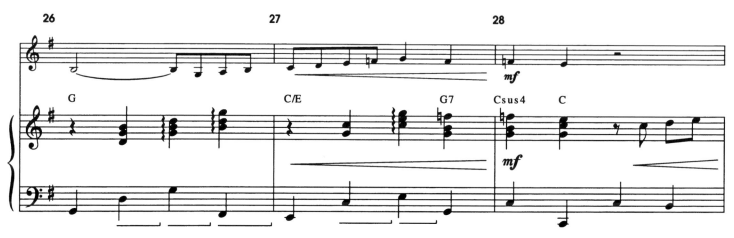

8. ALONG CAME A SPIDER

Mike Hannickel (ASCAP)

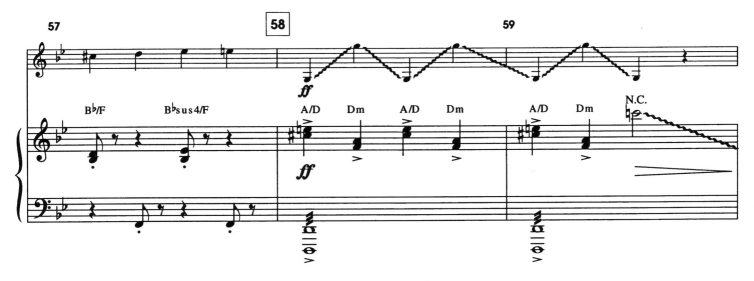

MALLET PERCUSSION

Leo Delibes
9. PIZZICATI from "SYLVIA"

Arr. **Ann Lindsay** (ASCAP)

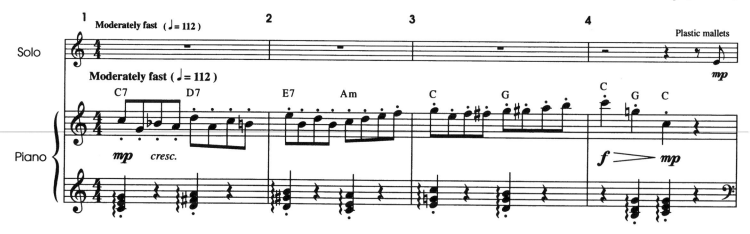

Copyright © 2003 by **Curnow Music Press, Inc.**

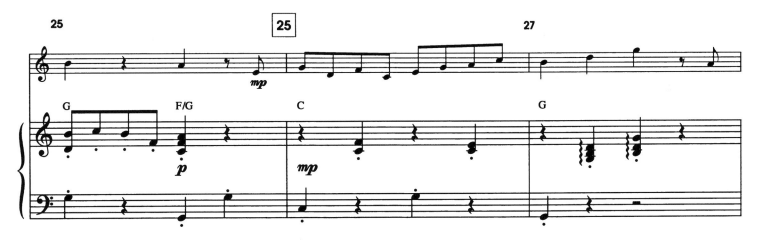

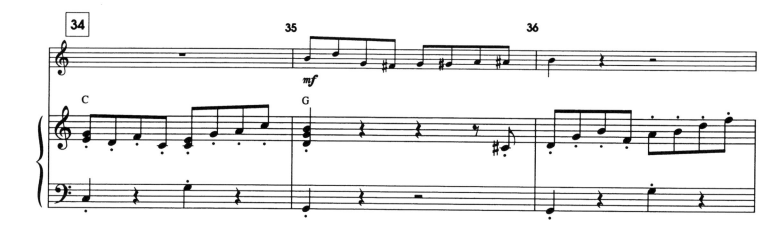

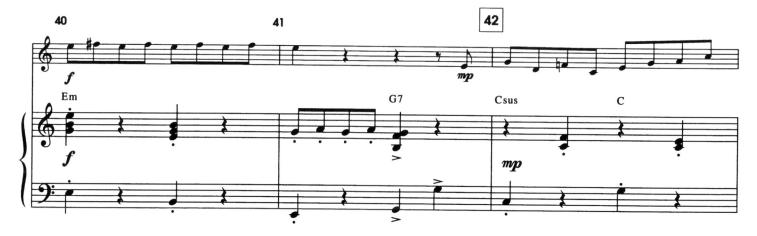

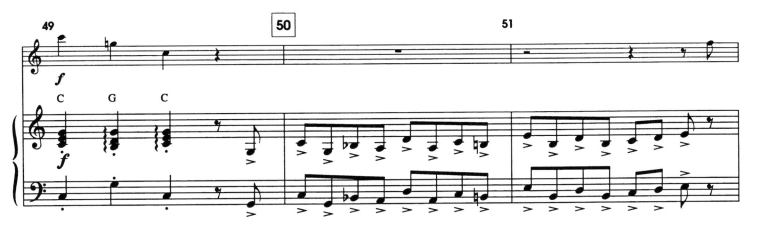

MALLET PERCUSSION

Charles Gounod

10. FUNERAL MARCH OF A MARIONETTE

Arr. **Ann Lindsay** (ASCAP)

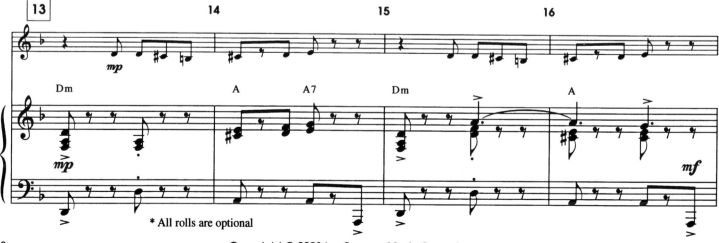

* All rolls are optional

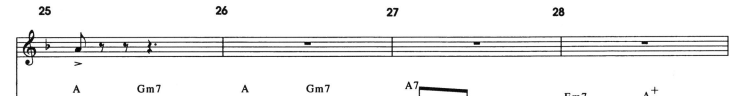

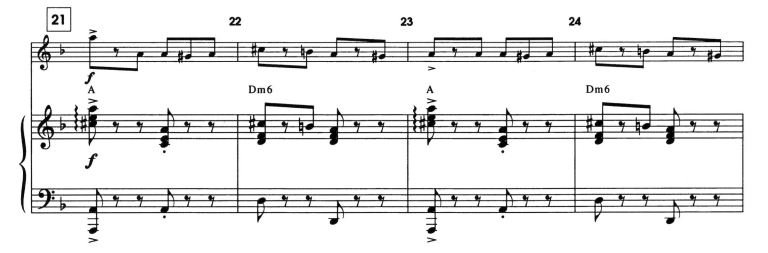

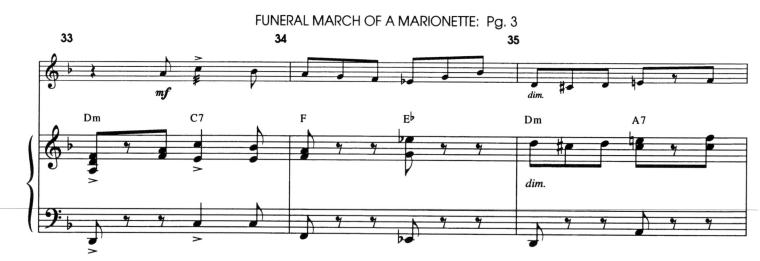

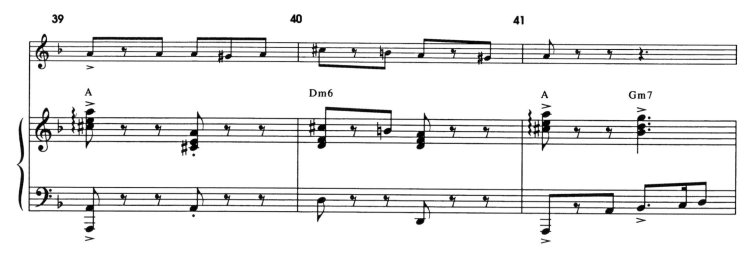

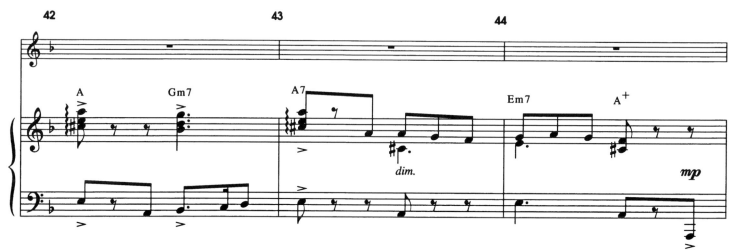

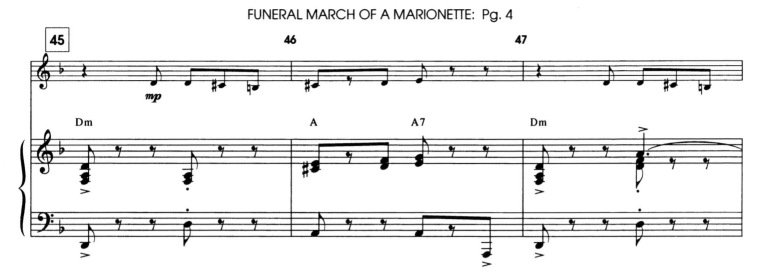

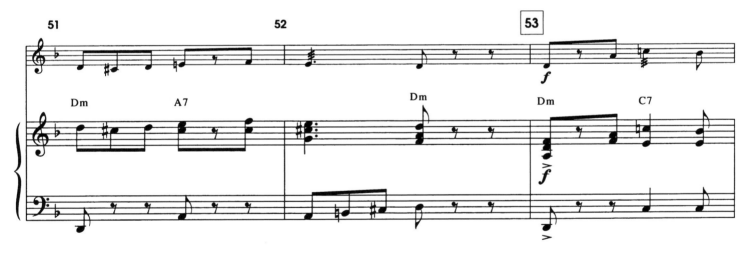

Alexander Borodin
Theme from
11. STRING QUARTET #2
"Nocturne"

MALLET PERCUSSION

Arr. **James Curnow** (ASCAP)

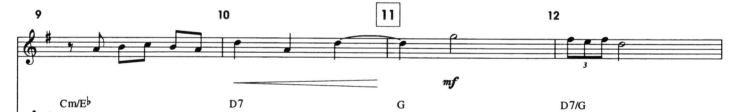

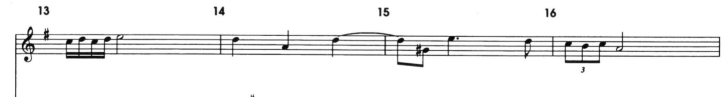

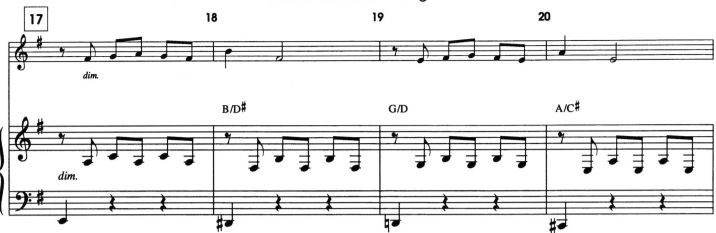

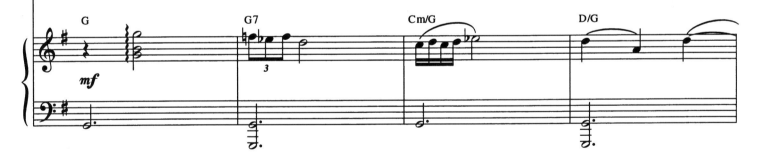

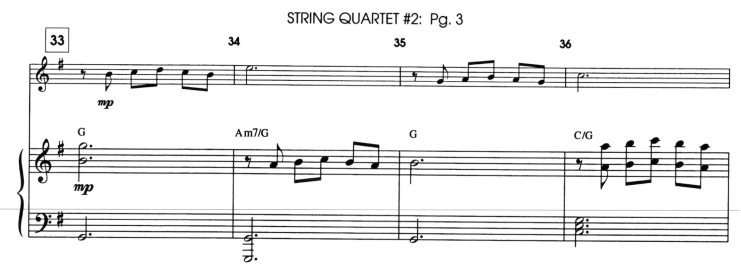

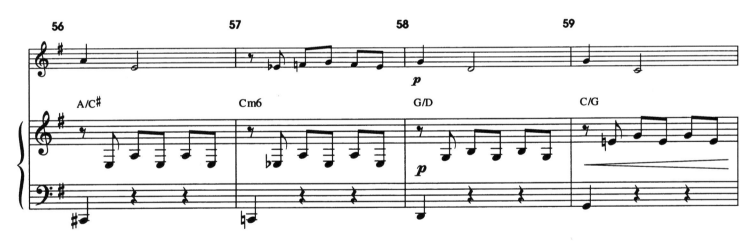

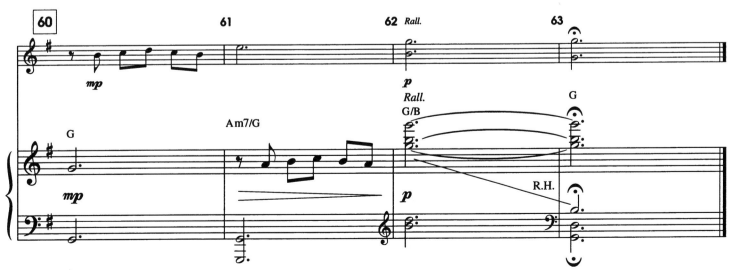

Jean Joseph Nouret

12. RONDEAU

Arr. **James Curnow** (ASCAP)

MALLET PERCUSSION

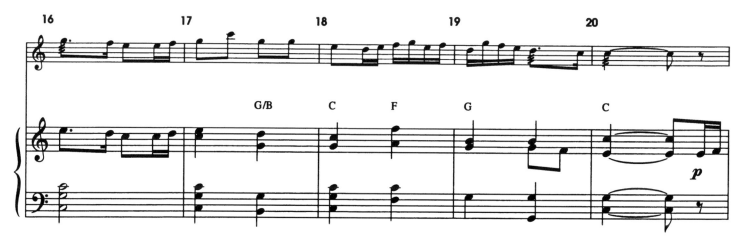

* All rolls are optional

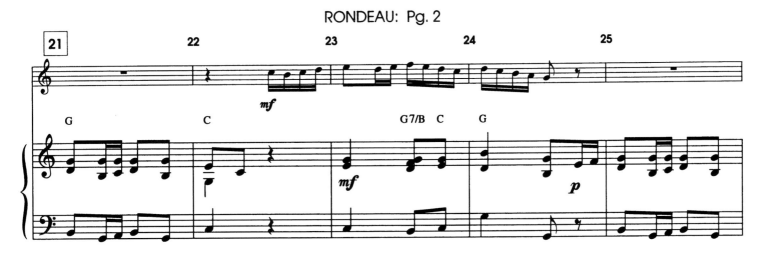

CMP 0857.03 Piano Acc. for Mallet Percussion